10 Scriptures on Joblessness That Can Change Your Life

Cole Johnson

COMI Publishing, Inc.
Cane Ridge, TN

Printed in the United States of America

Library of Congress Control Number: 2015930179

ISBN-13: 978-1507722855
ISBN-10: 1507722850

Published by:
COMI Publishing
Cane Ridge, TN 37013
www.comipublishing.com

Our mission is to provide content that inspires.

ACKNOWLEDGEMENTS

Almighty Father, I thank You for being with me when I was in the midst of an occupational desert. You provided for me when I was in a stage of unemployment. You then provided a way for me to build for my home. I thank You for sustaining me in those rough times – as well as the good ones. I love you, Jesus!

To the COMI Publishing, Inc. staff: Thank you so much for helping me put forth this message. In our conversations, it was mentioned that people need to hear encouragement in such a rough time. I tapped into my own experience and birthed this project. Thank you for your endless support.

To my life group: You all have been through different trials – as I have. We have helped each other persevere through them. I thank you guys for building me up when I was not at my best. Special thanks go to my brother, Scott, for praying this reaches those who struggle with unemployment on a daily basis.

To my wife, Michelle: Thank you for your patience in calamity. Thank you for your encouragement when my strength was depleted. Thank you for your strength when I was at my weakest. Thank you for your wisdom when I sought It (and even when I didn't seek it). I pray that I reward your wisdom, patience, strength and encouragement in due time. I love you so very much!

This book is dedicated to so many individuals who are in between jobs. No matter the time in your life, it is never easy to be in this season. However, know that if you keep your mind on God during this time, you will be rewarded for your diligence and steadfastness! Thank you for your patronage, and may God bless you in every endeavor!

3

Contents

BEGINNING THE PROCESS

A friend of mine mentioned in social media, *"Looking for a full-time job is a FULL-TIME job!"* No question about it.

Don't be afraid to ask God for what you want in a position. Then, when you receive it, seek Him (and all avenues God gives you) until you find it. Don't be afraid to knock on doors. Someone has to open it – and one of them has to say, *"Yes."* Know that God blesses the hands of other people to do His work, too. Don't simply look for 'the miracle sign', and, when you see nothing out of the ordinary, throw in the towel and do nothing. Someone needs you on their payroll.

Or ... you need yourself on your very own payroll. If you are in a season where your former was good – or even not so good – dig into God's purpose for you. There has to be something God blessed you to do to further His Gospel. There is a career with your name written all over it. You are possibly destined to be the boss. The saying goes, *"Pay the cost to be the boss."* Being terminated leads you to pay a heavy cost. Take this time to search and see if you are meant to also be an entrepreneur.

When you are applying to any job (newspaper, online, job sites, open solicitation, networking, etc.), know that the first thing God said to Adam was to prosper. Our Lord wants you to prosper. He has created you to be a king/queen over all the earth (in His Name, of course). You are purposely created to prosper. So refrain from thinking that your efforts mean nothing. They mean <u>everything</u> to all of us (including me). You are meant to contribute something. Always hunt for your position with that particular mindset.

Whatever you do – take time to lick your wounds. Your disappointment shows in job interviews. I remember one time, when I was an interviewer, I could literally sense disinterest in a candidate. Many of them dressed the part. A couple of them sounded the part. However, most of them weren't 'the part' because they were defeated before walking through the door. It is never pleasant to be fired, laid off or to have your contract expire. You owe it to your health to grieve. Say that not having a certain position hurts and that you want to still work at your last post. Once you let the grieving process take effect, prepare to be the best candidate for your next position.

Practice everything you can. Practice how you will sit in interviews. Practice what you will say. Practice how you will say it. Practice what you will wear. Practice the art of being in control and confident. Make it a part of your everyday habit until you land the position you desired. If you can do it, use positions at other industries as 'practice' for the job you truly want. You never know. You might hit a home run when you least expect it. Remember: The goal in an interview is not to show them how hungry you are in wanting a position. Desperation is the last thing interviewers/employers want to see. The goal is to demonstrate to them that you already belong in their culture. Make them see that it would be the worst decision they would make to have you walk out of their doors. Make it a point to know almost as much about the business as the ones sitting across from you. The more you stand out – and be yourself – the better your chances are in being hired.

And don't be afraid to practice in front of someone else, as well. That will also help you get better.

The reason why I can go so in-depth with those feelings is simple: I've endured the nasty sting of joblessness, myself. I felt all of those emotions – and more. I went through a stretch where I was unemployed for eight months. That's right – I said, *"Eight months."* I can't begin to tell you how helpless I felt in that time period. I went through Thanksgiving, Christmas, New Year's, Resurrection Sunday, and my own birthday sans a job. Imagine going through these times of celebration, and you personally don't have the spirit or the energy to do just that. It was the most humbling, and trying, time of my entire life.

However, it was also the most eye-opening moment of my life, as well.

Sometimes, we have to open our eyes to the prospect of something new. In the Bible's Book of 2 Kings, the prophet, Elisha, met with a widow who had a son and a mounting debt. His advice to her was simple, *"What do you have?"* She answered, *"Nothing but this pot of oil."* Elisha advised her to borrow as many oil flasks as she could – and, once she received them, to pour Into them until the oil in said pot ran empty. So, she rounded up those flasks and poured … and poured … and poured. Once the pot was empty, Elisha advised her to sell the oil. The widow sold so much of the oil that, not only did she pay off her debt, but she, and her son, had more than enough to comfortably live.

This brings the story of Chris Gardner to mind, or better known as *The Pursuit of Happyness* story. He was slated to be in the medical field, but became a medical sales representative, instead. Tough times and trouble followed him, and he was left searching for another career. One chance meeting with a stockbroker changed his fortunes. He was classified as homeless (with a two-year old son) for one year before being able to learn the ropes of being a stockbroker. Because of being jobless, Gardner discovered his career path and has built wealth for his children and his grandchildren (as we all are supposed to do).

As for me, I got back on my feet and worked a position. Along with that, I also discovered my gift of writing and decided, *"Now is the time to really do what I love ... and have no regrets."* Because of that, my life is richer and happier. It does make those days of doom and gloom distant in time – but it's not far from my memory.

So ... you're in the trenches of finding your way to a job. However, you're one of the, possible, 35 – 40 million unemployed Americans. You're looking for that 'light at the end of the tunnel' scenario. Well, when things get rugged in life, we have to simplify our focus. *"Easier said than done,"* right? Of course! However, it is necessary to do this at times in life.

For me, I tapped into the Word of God just to see what the Lord had to say about 'job hunting' and 'job losses'." As you're about to witness; He says a lot about it. The one constant thread that you will see (and I witnessed myself) is a mind transformation. Paul wrote to his fellow Romans saying, *"Do not conform to the pattern of this world, but be transformed by the renewing of your mind. Then you will be able to test and approve what God's will is – His good, pleasing and perfect will."*

Please take this time, right now, to find your purpose in God – because your breakthrough will be found at His fingertips.

#1 – Focus On The Future

ISAIAH 43:18-19

Isaiah Relays God's Mercy

<u>18</u> "Forget the former things; do not dwell on the past.

<u>19</u> See, I am doing a new thing! Now it springs up; do you not perceive it? I am making a way in the wilderness and streams in the wasteland."

One thing that is very easy to do for us is to dwell on what we did in the past. I had issues, going both ways, in learning this lesson. I would dwell on the past too much at times AND I would purposely forget the former things and not learn the lesson before putting said past behind me.

In both cases, all of us are doomed to repeat the same mistake.

If our focus is on the past thing, the future thing will slip right by our eyes. The word 'perceive' is a verb – and one of the definitions is, 'to become aware through the senses.' In the case of being jobless, this would imply seeing something new develop. It could be a job fair. It could be a missed call from an employer. It could be a book that could give you a new – or better – perspective on where you are. It also could be a solid opportunity to make money.

Even God said that He is making a way in the wilderness. That simply means the translation of an old-school church saying of, "*He can make a 'way' out of 'no way'*," comes to life. It requires us to pay attention to the way being made in the first place. Sometimes, that way being made is not necessarily the job, itself. It could be your circumstances, as well. There may be times when something comes from out of nowhere to help you through the rough season you're undergoing. It could be something temporary to hold you over until something more permanent happens. It also could be the friends and family who love you and want to see you win – and help you while you're in your valley.

That way in the wilderness – along with streams in the wasteland – demands us to do one thing: We have to tap into how God thinks/speaks/blesses. Is it hard to think that way? Of course! We look at the natural way of things. Jesus is about the supernatural view. Later in this Book, Isaiah was also told that God's ways are greater than ours as His thoughts are higher than ours.

So you must shift your way of thinking in order to grow into the next position that is destined for you. You must shift your eyes in the direction of Heaven in order to truly see what is out there for you. Stevie Wonder sang it so beautifully, *"When you feel your life is hard // just go have a talk with God // When your load's too much to bear // Talk to God, He really cares."* He really does care. He wants to know what you're thinking - what you're feeling - what you're suffering. God's desire is to create a new thing. That also means He wants to create that 'new thing' inside of you. That transformation will create the open opportunities to spring forth in a way you've never seen before.

#2 – The 'ASK' Principle

MATTHEW 7:7-12

Jesus Speaks About Pursuing What You Want

7 "Ask and it will be given to you; seek and you will find; knock and the door will be opened to you. 8 For everyone who asks receives; the one who seeks finds; and to the one who knocks, the door will be opened.

9 "Which of you, if your son asks for bread, will give him a stone? 10 Or if he asks for a fish, will give him a snake? 11 If you, then, though you are evil, know how to give good gifts to your children, how much more will your Father in heaven give good gifts to those who ask him! 12 So in everything, do to others what you would have them do to you, for this sums up the Law and the Prophets.

I'll admit; there are times when it seems that Jesus speaks in straight-up riddles. After all, we are meant to stretch our brain and think. He also was/is an effective teacher, as well – and the job of an instructor is to provoke thought beyond your present-day comprehension.

Then, there are times when Jesus just simply gives it to you straight. This is one of those times.

I used to sing this Scripture in a round back in my younger choir days. In that time, I simply thought it was merely words. I didn't quite understand that it was Jesus speaking these words to His disciples. Once I understood it, the words, obviously, took on a considerably heavier weight and meaning.

Now, *"what does this mean from a job standpoint,"* you ask? It is very simple: When we were children, and we wanted something, what did we do? We would ask our parents for it, right? If we wanted to have that Christmas toy, or that great shirt, or even to play in some extracurricular activity, we would ask/seek/knock on our parent(s) door for it.

If we are to do that with our parents while we were young, why are we failing to do that, now, as adults to the Lord? After all, God still regards us as His children.

In the middle of His Sermon on the Mount, Jesus, in a sense, lays out what it means to be a citizen of the Kingdom. He displayed what it meant to take up His cross and follow Him. Part of that life included asking God for clarity, seeking answers from God, and knocking until the Lord opened the door.

We walk through life not knowing what to do on our own. So, in order to understand our purpose, we have to ask questions. Remember: Back in school, teachers would tell us, *"There's no such thing as a dumb question – because the dumbest question is the one that goes not asked."* God feels the same way – especially when it comes to a job. We don't know what to do. Our journey in life is about two things:

1. Thanking God in creating us.
2. Discovering why He did.

The only way we are to know what it is we are meant to do on Earth is to ask questions. God wants us to ask these questions. He delights in giving us the answer to His purpose in us.

Then, there's the seeking part. You are good at certain things. Maybe you are wonderful with your hands and can build something. It's quite possible that you can cook better than most anyone. Your skill might be in public speaking. Maybe, your purpose to edify the Body of Christ is to sing all over the world. Whatever your gift may be, you owe it to yourself to seek God for the answer. It is imperative to seek, yourself, the answer, as well. I discovered writing when I was 14 years old. Most teenagers wanted to go to malls and shop. Some wanted to be with their friends. I wanted to sit at my desk and physically put pen to paper. I felt a peace that passed all sorts of understanding ... but I didn't know it. Remember, *"The one who seeks finds."*

Here is where the persistence comes into play. We all are meant to have someone else help us with the vision God gave us to execute. When it comes to a job offer, it takes many people to facilitate it to happen. When it comes to an entrepreneurial opportunity, it takes others to help execute the vision. In order to get where you're going, you have to continue to be persistent. You can't quit. Even if your hand bleeds from knocking too long or too much ... keep knocking. (Now, I know that image is rather graphic, but let's be real: Sometimes, getting what you want can be an exhausting pruning process.)

The same goes for employers/when you are becoming an employer. Your time is now in being blessed with provision. You can't have any other outlook. Imagine the end result, and go after it. It may take a while, but you are working toward that goal. Each breath you are taking is getting you closer to what you were created to do. You're asking God for His wisdom in every situation in your life. You are seeking after what God told you, and you are knocking on every door the Lord has given you to confront.

It's all about one thing: Jesus tells us to put the elbow grease in praying and doing.

Overall, God wants you to work. He wants you to provide for your families. He also wants you to provide for His Kingdom. There would be no way He would allow you to be sans an occupation. There is definitely no way he would want you to be devoid of a purpose. From the context of a job: This is meant for all of us to turn to the source that really matters. No one knows us better than the Father. He knows why He created us better than we do. So – if that's the case, shouldn't we ask the Lord what is our purpose on Earth? Shouldn't we ask questions about what it is we are meant to do? Shouldn't we seek to find it? Shouldn't we knock and expect the door to be opened?

Yes, we should – and the Lord delights in the fact we trust Him enough to do it. To know about how a certain thing operates, one must ask questions about it. There may be new techniques to discover in your job searching. There may be different businesses you haven't tried. In asking, seeking and knocking on the door to God, you will be closer to realizing the end of your occupational desert. It may be time to get creative and find new ways to earn a life - or the job to which you applied months ago is now ready to hire you. No matter what the scenario, your eyes have to be open, your ears have to be attentive and your heart must never grow despondent and bitter.

Focus on the light of God, and you will taste success in ways you never imagined.

#3 – Pulling On Supply

PHILIPPIANS 4:19

Paul Touches On Gifts

<u>19</u> And my God will meet all your needs according to the riches of his glory in Christ Jesus.

"We get caught in the trap of having to do it all by ourselves. There's no question that you have to put in the time – and the work – in order to get accomplished what needs to be done.

However, you don't have to go through the process alone.

One of the greatest, and most painful, lessons I had to learn was to let go of being in control of it all. One of the most oft-quoted sayings comes from a poem written by William Ernest Henley: *"I am the master of my fate // I am the captain of my soul."* As you have witnessed with a chaotic job market (and so have I), nothing could be further from the truth. Almost all of us have no idea what our fate entails (alone), and we certainly are not the captains of our souls. Both of those categories belong to God. Now, we can tap from God's wisdom what our fate may be, but we are most definitely not in control.

I also had to trust that others, who are in the Body of Christ along with me, would be part of the 'supply line' Paul mentions in his letter to the Philippians. When bad things happen, we have a tendency to become more and more reclusive. We don't want anybody to be around us until we are better. We are sure no one understands our pain (and in some cases, they don't). We are positive that no one will have the answer for what ails us (unless it's about a job opening). I'll talk about this later.

But God wants us to know that He has the supply waiting for you. All you have to do is apply The ASK Principle (ask, seek, knock). The Lord is a Father that wants you to be full of joy. He wants you to be prosperous. He wants you to bless this world with the gifts He gave you. That is utterly impossible if you are stuck in occupational neutral.

Recently, I attended a gathering of fellow Believers where the speaker said the following: *"For ten years … I earned a good living, but was miserable. Then, I received a job that barely paid half as much as the one before it, but I received more fulfillment(s) from it. The blessing that God placed on that particular job made not getting paid as much worth it because He stretched the money – and allowed us to save even more because of it. So sometimes, it's not always about the money, but it's about being in your assigned purpose."*

Truer words were never spoken.

I will add, though, that you should get paid what you're worth. The Lord does want to supply you with being a blessing on Earth. His desire is that you can turn around and utilize His blessings to touch other people's lives. Don't worry about your needs. Give all of that to God, and watch what He does in you.

#4 – The Importance of God's Righteousness

PSALM 37:23-26

David Sings of the Right Mindset

23 The Lord makes firm the steps of the one who delights in him;

24 though he may stumble, he will not fall, for the Lord upholds him with his hand.

25 I was young and now I am old, yet I have never seen the righteous forsaken or their children begging bread.

26 They are always generous and lend freely; their children will be a blessing.

It is hard out here to survive without a job. There is no question about it. After all, this society depends on the exchange of cash flow to make the world turn. Almost everything that is necessary for us to live on this earth costs something. So – a job is important. Of course, you feel low when that job is gone.

That's why it is important to still keep your eyes on God during this time.

However (and I love this), we shouldn't only ask for things like the Lord is some spiritual genie. He is a lot more than that. This Scripture talks about having the mindset of building up your righteousness. That's why it is written in the Book of Hebrews: *"And let us consider how we may spur one another on toward love and good deeds, and not giving up meeting together, as some are in the habit of doing, but encouraging one another – and all the more as you see the Day approaching."* Our friends in the Truth are meant to help pour into our spirit. When you are having moments of despair being unemployed, it is important to have those friends demonstrate why you are the righteousness of God. They will assist in making your hard times less unbearable.

Along with your friends, take time to work on yourself. What I mean by that is this: Work on becoming a better human being. It has been my experience that we, as humans, are more attentive to God when we are personally pained with something. Chances are that you may discover something unsavory about yourself that you need to change. It is all a part of building yourself to be in right standing with God.

When you get out of your situation, you may look back at that time period and realize you were sustained by the Lord. You couldn't explain the type of provision in such a rough time to a non-Believer. To those who do believe in the power of the Trinity, on the other hand, we would exchange knowing glances and smiles. I've been there, and was not forsaken by Him.

You won't be forsaken, either. I know it looks bleak, but hold on and continue in your search to how God gives you provision for your family. Imagine yourself employed. Now do the work necessary to get that particular position. Until then, work on you. Make God rejoice and show Him that, even in such a rough time, He can still delight in you. You can do it!

#5 – You Are An Overcomer

JOHN 16:33

Jesus Prepares Disciples for His Death

<u>33</u> "I have told you these things, so that in me you may have peace. In this world you will have trouble. But take heart! I have overcome the world."

We can draw inspiration from human life in different arenas. We find that the most enthralling stories are people who have gone through turmoil to find grand success. Many stories from figures we respect come from those who have used their down moments as fuel for their ultimate success.

Steve Jobs is a great example of this. Here is a man who co-founded the computer company, Apple. The company experienced early success but experienced a harsh downturn when the market became more competitive. Because of it, Apple fired him as CEO. For over a decade, he was away from what he did best – and what he loved. He didn't quit. He kept going – and eventually found his way back to Apple. Then, after stabilizing the company he founded, Jobs spearheaded iPhone, iPad, and iTunes. He was transformed from a person who was considered a dinosaur to that of a technological rock star. Whatever he (literally) pitched made Apple not only cutting edge, but financially successful – beyond their projections. His struggle made him better – and his success made Jobs relatable to us.

Many people speak of one of our presidents, Abraham Lincoln, as one of the hallmark commanders-in-chief the United States has ever had. However, in 1854 – and again in 1858 – Lincoln lost two United States senatorial campaigns. It was in large part because he was a candidate against slavery at a time when the politics still leaned a little heavier toward the institution being an accepted way of life. Politics, today, is big business. Whenever we have seen high profile candidates lose campaigns, there has been a stigma placed onto them (fair or unfair). Lincoln faced similar pressures before throwing his hat in the presidential ring. He could have let the failures stop him from aspiring to a higher office. Lincoln pressed forward instead – eventually being elected to two terms as president. If he were to have let the bitter defeats stop him, we wouldn't have had one of the greatest examples of a strong head of state to use as an example, today.

Then, there is the woman who was born into a teenage single mother family. She also suffered from abuse and gave birth to a son at the age of 14 (who died in infancy) herself. She even wore dresses made of potato sacks. That woman is now an international media conglomerate all by herself. The woman to whom I'm referring is Oprah Winfrey.

Now you have to ask yourself these questions:

- Why is he talking about these things not fully relating to a job, per se?
- What do all of these stories mean?
- How can I apply this to my life?

The answer to all three of these questions is this: Through life, you are going to struggle. Struggling, for any human being, is like breathing. None of us like it (but we do love breathing). All of us wish we could prosper without going through growing pains. Many of us even receive wisdom – and still learn lessons the hard way, instead. Today, the job climate is unstable - and the workforce subscribing to a more transitory portfolio. Combine that with a volatile economy and inner panic is bound to spread. In today's business world, there are more layoffs, more business foreclosures, more mergers and more outsourcing which exists. The obstacles can be insurmountable – if you only focus on them … instead of your divine path.

What so many people have learned is something they may (or may not) believe, themselves, but is the result of exactly what happened. Somewhere in their life's journey, they discovered the source of their success (or 'secret') comes from a Savior who has taken challenges and rose above them. Jesus was a radical – plain and simple. He wasn't about the status quo. He was about showing the way to live this life on Earth. He showed that it was more than just talking the talk. We all have to walk the walk. He showed that relationship is the most important aspect of any bond. And, in His Death, Resurrection and Ascension, Jesus most certainly proved that He could overcome anything thrown at Him and be stronger for it.

If that energy is within Jesus (and Jesus resides within us) then that means we are overcomers, too. The world can tell us that an idea is bad. The world can display that what you have planned is considered stupid. The world can even prove by statistics and history that you will fall flat on your face and fail. We can walk with the belief that we won't ever find a job that is suitable – ever! We even accept it when the world says that we are only supposed to be Just Over Broke – working a 9-to-5. The only way to truly make it, I've heard the world say, is to give up your life and being a slave to work. I don't think so!

Part of being an overcomer is not only being bold enough to roll up your sleeves and grind – but working smart. There are gifts God gave every one of us. We do Him (and I did Him) a disservice by not knowing them. We do an even greater disservice to Him if we know what those gifts are – and sit on them (guilty as charged there, too)! Paul said that many of us in the Church have different talents – but all of them are meant to glorify the Lord and advance the Gospel to all corners of the world. In order for that to happen, it would mean you would have to expand your mind extending far beyond a simple commute to an occupation. It means investing time in your gifts and seeing how it blesses others. If you find a gift that blesses others, then you owe it to God – and yourself – to properly build on that gift. That's how Oprah Winfrey found communications. That's how Steve Jobs found technology. That's how Abraham Lincoln, being a wrestler and a lawyer, found politics. They tapped into the gifts God gave them – and it helped them overcome all the naysayers which surrounded them.

You can overcome every 'no' anyone tells you. You have a gift to bless this world. The divinely blessed gift will lead you to gather more influence than you could ever imagine. Yours will be that story which will make us drop our jaws and say, *"Oh my Lord! Look at what this person overcame to succeed the way they did!"* Riches are in you, and so is being an overcomer. Thank you, Jesus, for those gifts!

#6 – Grieve The Loss

REVELATION 21:4

John Writes About a New Day

4 "He will wipe every tear from their eyes. There will be no more death' or mourning or crying or pain, for the old order of things has passed away."

I was hard at work ... looking for work. *"I was going to be productive,"* I thought as I searched for some ray of hope. My wife must have seen something about me that was not quite right that day. She stopped what I was doing and asked for me to talk with her. I found it more and more difficult to even engage in a conversation about this particular subject at the time.

Then – it happened. I cried for nearly 10 solid minutes. The floodgates opened and the tears simply flowed. I can describe the feeling in vivid detail: I thought something was profoundly wrong with me as I was breathing, but not working. At this time, I applied to different places – and different industries – to hear no response (even after following up with them). I felt completely out of sorts – away from my purpose. I was thoroughly embarrassed (with no longer having my last position and searching so hard for one). I didn't realize that I emotionally pushed aside the pain in order to function as 'normal'.

It is like losing a loved one to death. You've invested enough time to build memories. There's an element that you want these good times to last. Then, in an instant, your world changes with the condition of loss. Many of us are taught that you keep moving forward without shedding tears. After all, this world doesn't like 'crybabies'. *"There are no time for tears – suck it up,"* as the saying goes.

Well - since Jesus overcame the world, that particular rule doesn't apply. In fact, Jesus wants us to cry when we are affected by such catastrophic events in our lives. Besides, how can the Lord wipe tears from our eyes if we choose not to cry, at all? Normally, when any of us cry, it is a sign that we need to release something. It is a clear-cut admission to everyone (including the Lord) that we can't handle whatever is stressing us, anymore. However, grieving, as a whole, can be a chore.

It certainly was a chore for me. After the cry, though (and prayer), I felt lighter and better. It also opened up new possibilities for me to pursue other options. It freed my mind. It set free my spirit. It renewed my soul. Bottom line is that grieving the loss of a job is a natural, normal behavior – and it is something you must do in order to properly put the sting of the act behind you.

This also leads to God wiping those tears from your eyes. In other words: Grieving leads to comfort. Comfort leads to clarity. Clarity leads to renewed energy and purpose. Give yourself permission to grieve – because God wants to bring His provision to you. It gives Him the opportunity to remind you that you are great (because He is even greater, and dwells within you). He can whisper to your ear that your purpose on this earth is long from finished. He can show you that your life is spectacular – and will be even more amazing. He does all that while your old life passes away.

#7 – Get/Stay Prepared

2 TIMOTHY 2:15

Paul Advises Timothy on Preparation

<u>15</u> Do your best to present yourself to God as one approved, a worker who does not need to be ashamed and who correctly handles the word of truth.

You must be prepared – no matter what.

This situation is not unlike being an understudy of a big-time Broadway show. You could be sitting on the sideline for a good long while. You are nothing more than a spectator. All of a sudden – something unfortunate could happen to the starting actor/actress, and you are inserted onto the stage. You are charged with upholding the standard previously set by your predecessor.

Just like a Broadway understudy - in the game of life, you always have to be ready. There is no telling when you will get called for a job interview. You can't predict when you'll hear the words, *"You're hired."* You certainly don't know who you'll impress – and who you won't. We can agree that none of us can predict when our employment drought ends. However, we can aid in its haste … by preparation.

When I was on the job hunt, I went to interviews early (when I was freshly hurt from being fired) with the pain evident. I went through the motions. I gave answers I thought would-be employers wanted to hear. I actually thought landing the interview were victories. With the advice I received from my wife, I had to change my strategy and approach. I prepared doing interviews in my house. I studied things which would make me a better candidate. I even went back to the notes I took when I was an interviewer years before. All of these things helped me to become a better prospect to get hired. There were times I actually took certain interviews simply to polish my skills.

It all led to this one particular multi-pronged interview process. There were two phone interviews, then a face-to-face interview. I was composed, yet personable in the introductory phone interview. I was all-business, yet teeming with personality with my second phone interview (while I was loading my car with groceries at the same time). By the time I got to the face-to-face interview – I was the most prepared to be in front of this three-person panel than at any time. In doing research for being a memorable interviewee, I read that you must do something to stand out in interviews. What I used to become memorable to the interviewers was the 'weapon' of humor. I used the humor to open the door, and went with honesty the rest of the way. I also learned that you must study about the company for which you are interviewing. I did that, too, and threw in a tidbit about the company in said interview. I was so impressive to the panel that I was hired only three hours after the interview was over.

It is all about preparation. In the Christian realm, the research starts with the Bible. It continues with individuals who also know the Word of God. This verse talks about being diligent in research, preparation and discipline. It takes all of these traits to greatly succeed in the Kingdom.

What means so much to an organization looking for new employees is the fact that you take the time to prepare for the new position. Sit at the seat of an owner for a second. Who would you want to hire: A person who simply went through the motions, answered questions and showed no interest in your business? Or would you want someone who walks in the door and shows they may know as much about your company as you do while being personable to boot? That's what I thought. If you owned a business and wouldn't want to invest your time, energy and resources on someone who shows little to no interest upon your first glance – then you can't be that type of would-be employee to an employer, either. This is why preparation is important. It will expedite your time on the unemployed sidelines while you wait for the "*You're hired*" go ahead from a company.

Understand – looking for a job is an occupation unto itself. That does mean looking in ads. That does mean calling in favors (if possible). That does mean stepping outside your comfort zone, at times. It also means strategizing to make it all possible. What I personally learned was this: The more disciplined your search, the better (and more productive) your process. I can't stress enough that vulnerability (the right kind) is part of the preparation process, as well. God doesn't want your representative in studying to show yourself approved for whatever blessing He wants to release in you. He wants to see that you are doing the work – willing to openly receive whatever blessings He gives you.

The same premise goes with job searches. I used to think that companies wanted someone who was hungry and desperate. That's not what companies want. They want a person who has already assumed the position before they step in the door to greet whoever influences the hiring process. When you diligently study the Word of

God, how do you feel: Do you feel lost, confused and unsure of yourself when it comes to the Word? Or do you feel emboldened, strong, confident, assured of yourself and solid in the understanding that the Lord is true and everything else is a lie? You would be a warrior for God (like we're supposed to be), right? Well, God wants us to be warriors, as well, when it comes to job preparation!

Think long and hard about when you are not prepared for a situation. There's trepidation. There's hesitation. There's doubt. There's anxiety. When any person is nervous, hesitant, doubtful and anxious, then we are out of our element – period. Part of the interview process is to see how well you would do under certain types of pressure. Interviewers know that it's a nerve-wracking process. I'm sure many of them probably could relate to the times when they were sitting in that same seat, themselves. Imagine you are attending the interview process (which is a pressure cooker, as it is), and you're nervous, hesitant, doubtful and anxious. I can tell you from experience … it doesn't go well.

Now – think long and hard about being prepared. If you are to not be anxious about anything, but, with prayer and thanksgiving, give your petitions to God – and watch His peace (which passes all understanding) wash over your mind/heart/soul and spirit – the result would be different. You'd walk into that same interview composed, assured, confident and peaceful. You researched the position. You did homework on what makes you stand out amongst dozens of other hopefuls – and you trusted in the Lord (and didn't lean to your own understanding). Success can only abound when you study to show yourself approved. You have work to do. Properly research how you're going land your next avenue of provision – and watch your preparation pay dividends.

#8 – Searching For Your Purpose

GENESIS 2:15

God Instructs Adam to Work

15 The Lord God took the man and put him in the Garden of Eden to work it and take care of it.

For those who follow the Bible, this passage goes onward to state that Adam was free to eat from any tree in the garden save one.

However, the focus, here, is the mindset of purposeful work. Adam is the first man on the earth. He was put to work. He had a purpose – and he set out to do it. We all are no different from Adam inasmuch as we all have a purpose God has given us. We must set out to do it – no questions asked.

Here is the reason why I am using this Scripture: Talk to someone who loves what they do for a living. Really ask the questions as to why they look forward to getting up every day and do something that, quite honestly, you couldn't see yourself doing. The answers may surprise you. The Temptations' own Melvin Franklin said about singing, "*I would do this for free because I love it so much.*"

The key to that is when someone is in their purpose, it no longer is considered laborious to them. It's considered a labor of love. You are a more valued asset to your employer (or, if you're blessed in this particular season, you are a more valued asset to yourself), and time seems to go by faster. Comedian Chris Rock did a funny bit on the difference between working at a job you dislike vs. a job you love. He deduced that time 'drags' at a job you don't like, whereas, in a job you love, you don't have nearly enough time in the day to complete all the tasks – and the time 'goes by faster'.

I know what you're saying, "*Well, I need to get a job, now – doing anything! How does this apply?*" I have been there. I know what you're feeling. Think of many different business executives and entertainers who you know – and almost all of them had humble beginnings. Some of them had a crossroads moment (like you are having, right now). They knew it was their purpose to work ... at something they loved to do. Along with finding something to pay the bills, focus, as well, on something you love to do – and put it out there to the masses. Who knows? One day, something that rated as only a hobby could turn into the provision where your cup runs over. Rock & Roll Hall of Fame songwriter, Kenny Gamble, said it this way: "*Always do something that will put the food on the table. Continue to work on what you love, and hone your craft, until it pays for your living. Don't put off your dream, but don't be irresponsible in your pursuit of it, either.*"

It's all in the purpose. The Lord is taking you, right now, to His garden and put you to work. Your mission is to walk in this 'garden', find out what exactly it is you were blessed to do in it – and get busy. So, in this time of looking for employment, know what type of work God wants you to do.

In the end: You'll be more apt to take care of things and even prosper from it.

#9 – Put In Productive Work

2 THESSALONIANS 3:6-10

Paul Instructs Against Idleness

6 In the name of the Lord Jesus Christ, we command you, brothers and sisters, to keep away from every believer who is idle and disruptive and does not live according to the teaching you received from us. 7 For you yourselves know how you ought to follow our example. We were not idle when we were with you, 8 nor did we eat anyone's food without paying for it. On the contrary, we worked night and day, laboring and toiling so that we would not be a burden to any of you. 9 We did this, not because we do not have the right to such help, but in order to offer ourselves as a model for you to imitate. 10 For even when we were with you, we gave you this rule: "The one who is unwilling to work shall not eat."

Think back in your past to anybody who poured into you. It can be anyone in your life. For most of us, it would be our parents. Now, for many of you who have since grown to become parents, yourselves: What is your particular posture about pouring into your children's lives? If they have become adults, themselves: How did you feel when you felt they squandered what you taught them? Then you can relate to Paul's warning, right here, with those who lived in the city of Thessalonica.

Paul is saying, *"We've modeled the way for you. We gave you examples. It's up to you, to take the ball and run with it."*

The very first verse hits home to lot of you out there (especially those who are just out of college – or even high school). There are those of you who can relate to hanging around certain individuals who simply don't have your best interest at heart. Their character, to be kind, is suspect. Part of their character flaw is that they are spiritually idle. In other words: They are not active in putting the Word of God in them. So – elements may be introduced to delay, disrupt or downright derail whatever progress you may have made in working toward a better life.

If we are to not be around those who are idle – then what about us? The saying definitely goes for us, as well. It's a true saying, "*If you gon' do nuthin', then you gon' git' nuthin'.*" Being sans a job does not give any of us a license to take a life vacation. It is tempting. Believe me, I was in that mindset. However, my life didn't dictate to me that I could take a day off from finding something that would fulfill my household. Pastor Creflo Dollar said something profound once about this: "*For those who say you don't need money to make you happy and maintain peace; go about two months without money or a job. I guarantee that you won't be happy knowing those bills keep comin'. Your peace is evaporated.*"

I'm sure you also have heard many adults say to you when you were younger, "*No one's gon' hand you nuthin'.*" That's true. If you mine a life-affirming situation, then you might get 'handed' something. Of course what I mean by 'handed' is simply this: You may actually network – and one day, when you least expect it, you receive that fateful phone call to the provision which will propel you out of the unemployment doldrums. Networking is a form of working, as well. This also is an enemy of idleness.

Today's climate is much easier to contact other individuals in different assortment of ways; e-mail, social media and networking parties to name a few. There is no one way to secure that ideal position. However, the Scripture should be motivational enough for you to intelligently do *something*. Any strategic forward momentum should bring you one step closer to being employed once again.

Many quote this Scripture saying, "*If you don't work, you don't eat* (2 Thessalonians 3:10)." Although that can be true, it's not the accurate connotation of the verse. It looks good on a T-shirt (and I've seen it printed on them), but the message is rather callous if God would say it that way. Since He expressed it in a different way, it's not the act that is important. It is the intent in your heart to work which is the Lord's main concern. The concern is if you are willing to put in the (sometimes) blood, sweat and tears to get the job done. His concern is if you have a heart ready to better this place in which we temporarily reside. If the answer in your heart is, "*Yes,*" then your will has to transfer into executing an intelligent, God-given plan (see Habakkuk 2:2 for further information).

You have to settle within your heart that working is a principle of God. We work to survive. We work to improve on things (starting with ourselves). We work to provide for those who are less fortunate. We also work to spread the Gospel of Our Lord and Savior, Jesus Christ, as well. It is impressed upon us – from the first ever man – to work. That's why it is essential for us to be willing to 'get our hands dirty'. The reason why work is so important to God is because it gives us purpose. In doing work, we find ourselves normally getting close to what His will Is for us. The only way we get there is to invest in the mindset of production.

If you are a man, then I know you appreciate it when you hear a woman who's close to you say, "*I love a hard-working man.*" That's not a saying. That is a general principle almost all women respect. What is a huge complaint you hear most unsatisfied women say in regards to the romantically-inclined men in her life? "*He doesn't want to work.*" It's not that you are unemployed (and yes, that's stressful), but you can't compound the difficulty by throwing in the towel and quitting on life. In the Book of James, he talks about how perseverance has to finish its work so that, when the trial is over, you wouldn't lack anything. The reason why he phrased it that way was so that you can find an appreciation for your current struggle. And, when it's over, you learned a treasure trove of lessons along the way to improve yourself.

What I had to discover was that focused, strategized activity kept my mind from being idle. My father has said this to me countless times, and I didn't believe him until I went through being jobless: "*An idle mind is the devil's workshop.*" Translation: If you don't keep yourself busy, then you'll give the devil permission to wreak havoc on your thoughts. To keep this tendency at bay, Paul instructs the Corinthians (and, by proxy, all of us) to take captive of every thought and make it obedient to Christ. Since we are God's hands, feet, eyes, mouth, heart and brain, God wants us be willing to help this world become better. That cannot happen if you are unwilling to actually roll up your sleeves – and work.

Business sales guru, Dale Carnegie, once said the following: "*Inaction breeds doubt and fear. Action breeds confidence and courage. If you want to conquer fear, do not sit home and think about it. Go out and get busy.*" Don't be afraid to work. We depend on you to make a difference in this world.

#10 – Never Give Up

GALATIANS 6:9

Paul Writes of Doing Good

<u>9</u> Let us not become weary in doing good, for at the proper time we will reap a harvest if we do not give up.

Let's understand it for what it really is: You hear whispers that, "*You aren't good enough. Nobody wants you. You have nothing to offer. Everybody's more qualified. You're overqualified. You're not the right fit. You don't have enough education. You have too much education. You don't stand out. You stand out too much. You don't have the right attitude. You might as well throw in the towel. It's time to quit and resign yourself to the fact that you are forever receiving the short end of the stick.*"

Here's where you would be wrong.

There is a picture that depicts exactly what this Scripture says. There are two guys digging in a cave for a treasure den of diamonds. Each man is holding a rock pick in their hands. Each man has come a mighty long way to get to the diamond stash. The top gentleman is seen with the axe over his shoulder and walking away from the pile because he quit digging further. The bottom gentleman dug until the diamonds were discovered. The overarching message is this: You may be closer to your breakthrough than you think. Just because the road to get there is rough (or it's taking longer than to your liking) doesn't mean you'll be denied a reward. More often than not; if the journey is tougher, the reward is greater.

Keep grinding. Keep pushing. Keep going. Don't stop. The reason why I'm stating this to you is simple: There are more and more of us who taste the sting of unemployment. It is our spiritual duty to provide for our families and the world. God wants us to be prosperous – and that takes a lot of hard work in order to get there. The Lord knows you're going to run into some road bumps. Job said it: *"Mortals born of a woman are of few days and full of trouble."* He knows we are going to run into some difficulty in life. However, this is the time where you put even more trust in God to see you through and provide for you along the way. Then, you make trusting in Him a lifestyle (Romans 12:2).

It's quite scary to not have your hand on the steering wheel of life, isn't it? Go ahead and nod because I've been there! We want to dig ourselves out of holes, but we must realize that God wants to get a message to us. Sometimes, His message has to get through to us with little or no distractions. Is it stressful to go a while without a job? Of course it is! Somehow, some way, God will supernaturally provide for you along the way so that your focus is what He wants you to do. Eventually, this moment of hard times will bless you – and plenty of other people. All you have to do is keep the faith, and continue to do good. In the end, your perseverance will be thoroughly rewarded with a great harvest.

A friend of mine puts it this way, *"Don't practice quitting – or you'll become a professional."* No matter what the signs in your life's road dictate – keep going until your provision comes. Then – keep going!

FINAL WORDS OF WISDOM

This condition causes extreme anxiety.

It can affect the worst, and even the best, of us.

It can leave you doubting yourself at every turn.

What is this 'it' to which I'm referring? The 'it' is joblessness.

The following words may ring hollow to you if you are, at the present moment, without a job … but it is true: There is a job out there with your name all over it. The beautiful part about life is this: We go through storms. However, just like the ones we see outside – the storms have to end at some time. In the summer, rains can pour down as if there's no end in sight. In the winter, you can witness a blizzard – to the point where the atmosphere looks all white. If you're in it, you think, *"There's no way I can survive this."* When it's over, you question the sudden end to something so powerful. The storms in life work the same way. It can pour like the negativity will never end. Then, all of a sudden – as quickly as it arrived, it's over. The sunshine and rainbows in your life come rushing back to usher you into a season of harvest and good fortune.

"Yeah, but I'm going through, though," you say. I totally understand your pain my brother/sister.

You have attempted many techniques that have been given to you. You've knocked on doors. You've gathered job interviews. You've called businesses. You've even stepped outside your own field just to earn a paycheck … somewhere. If somebody … anybody … can just answer that key phone call, pass along the hope of a better tomorrow or shake your hand and say, *"You're hired,"* the burden of helplessness would subside for you. Sometimes, you'll go back and apply to your previous companies just to survive.

You just need to see at least ONE thing that's positive to result in your life. You want to cling onto something to let you know that you are not a failure. You need to know that victory is around the corner. You need to know that, 'trouble don't last always,' applies to your life, too – and you can see it for yourself.

That feeling of emptiness could all disappear with one scenario: All you need to do is hear that one, "Yes," from somebody. You crave to hear something positive that will put you back on your purpose. You need to see life get back to normal. Because we all know that – job or no job – the bills keep coming. We all know that – job or no job – the sun still rises and sets. We all know that – job or no job – the world keeps going, and others' lives don't stop for yours.

But that one, "Yes," can take a while. It makes you feel lost in this world if you don't hear it. It makes you feel inadequate. It makes you feel insignificant. It makes you doubt yourself. It can make you bitter. It can make you depressed. You definitely feel oppressed as you think about times you were on top of the world. Now – you feel the world is on top of you. If you're a woman, this feeling can be devaluing. If you're a man, this feeling is emasculating.

Strategize every aspect of your job search. Earlier, I expressed that looking for a job has to be a full-time job in and of itself. Plan your whole day (starting with when you awake), and go throughout the day. I used a method of writing a list and scratching through all that I accomplished. You will find that the more organized you are in your search, the more productive you will be. Remember: Job searches are not a game of darts – where you throw an apparatus at a position. There has to be a plan there, too. Solomon said, *"Many are the plans in a person's heart, but it is the Lord's purpose that prevails."* We are meant to write down that vision of ours and make it plain. Give your plan to God and watch how He will bless you.

Envision nothing but success. There is something about positive thinking that helps us all through every danger. Better yet, Paul wrote, *"... be transformed by the renewing of your mind."* The world speaks death every single moment. God speaks life at every turn. Thus, He wants us to shape our thinking to be more like Him. He wants you blessed, full of joy, and prosperous. When you see a successful person – what is their stance? They are blessed, full of joy, and (most definitely) prosperous! You are successful.

Your unemployment is a temporary situation. You are built to overcome every situation thrown at you. You can do all things through Christ who strengthens you. Say this every day in the mirror: *"I am Blessed. I am Prosperity. I am Success. I am an Overcomer."* Say it until you believe it. Then say it until you live it. As David sang, *"... Weeping may last through the night, but joy comes in the morning."*

Father God, in the Name of Jesus:

Your Word is the very fabric of purpose and prosperity. Thank You, Father, for Your purpose. May it shower through every single individual reading this book. May the wisdom You imparted fall on fertile soil, take root and grow in their hearts. Thank You Jesus for healing every single person who has been affected with the disappointment, embarrassment and shame of losing a job. Direct their eyes toward You at this time, for Your Word says, "*You will be kept in perfect peace those whose minds are steadfast, because they trust You.*" It is Your peace, Your grace and Your love that will be what leads these wonderful people of God to the work You have chosen for them to do.

Also, Father God – strengthen every single child of Yours as they search for positions. May their hands be more fruitful - may their minds be sharper – may their feet walk more in line with Your purpose than ever before. I pray for a supernatural protection over them. Encamp Your angels around them, Father, so that a thousand may fall at their side, ten thousand at their right hand, but the enemy will not come near them. Seal them with the Holy Spirit so that they receive Your blessings on a continual basis.

Guide them to the position built for them to prosper! I joyfully and humbly ask this, and rejoice that it is already done … in Jesus' Name – Amen!!!

I love you, Brothers and Sisters of the Truth!

About the Author

Cole Johnson was born in New Orleans and reared in Houston. After serving in the Army, his renewed faith enhanced his gift for writing. Along with the *10 Scriptures* series, he has been a contributor to several publications and calls Nashville home with his wife, Michelle.

For booking or additional help, write to Cole Johnson:

c/o COMI PUBLISHING; contact@comipublishing.com

NOTES

NOTES

NOTES

www.ingramcontent.com/pod-product-compliance
Lightning Source LLC
Chambersburg PA
CBHW071140280526
45787CB00003B/1350